C000127038

Sculptum Est Prosa

VOLUME 4

Also by Ivan Kireevskii

Sculptum Est Prosa

VOLUME 4

THE VOICES OF
THE OCEANS AND TREES

(poems of climate change)

Poetry by

IVAN KIREEVSKII

LUMINARE PRESS

WWW.LUMINAREPRESS.COM

Sculptum Est Prosa (Volume 4):
The Voices of the Oceans and Trees
(poems of climate change)
Copyright © 2020 by Ivan Kireevskii

All rights reserved. This book or any portion thereof may not be
reproduced or used in any manner whatsoever without the express
written permission of the publisher, except for the use of
brief quotations in a book review.

Printed in the United States of America

Cover Design by Claire Flint Last

Luminare Press
442 Charnelton St.
Eugene, OR 97401
www.luminarepress.com

LCCN: 2020907239
ISBN: 978-1-64388-374-8

For my grandchildren,
Jordan, Jonathan, Cameron, Emery, Evan, Erin
and great grandson, Jaylen

Contents

"But as a wintry globe descends precipitant...foot a black cloud redounding spread over Europe deform'd into indefinite space...All fell towards the Center in dire ruin, sinking down. And in the South remains a burning fire: in the East, a void: In the West, a world of raging waters: in the North, a solid. Unfathomable, without end."

—William Blake

As I submit this book to my publisher, the world sits on the precipice of social unrest, economic uncertainty and a pandemic of historic proportions. We are at a place as a civilization that has up to now been only conjured in the works of fiction. But here we are. I have to ask, how much of this has been brought due to our own selfishness, greed and total disregard for our planet and the plight of our sentient kin and one another?

Foreword

What is *Sculptured Prose?*

It is the descriptive title I have given to the style of poetry that I write. On my website: www.sculturedprose.com it states the following regarding my first book: *Sculptum Est Prosa—The Voices of Genius:*

> "*Astronomers peer into the heavens, mathematicians devise elaborate theories, physicists construct complex machines, and philosophers search for the ultimate answers and indeed, the ultimate questions…*
>
> *[My] poems are haunted by their voices…in which their words have been sculptured to harmonize.*"

Imagine a sculptor walking along the beach, through the forest, or climbing a mountain in search of a desirable stone with the potential to be chiseled and carved into a work of art. As I read and listen to the geniuses of our current age and past, I search their words just as a literal sculptor does his stones…once found, he or she carves, chisels, shapes, molds and fashions them with artistry and precision.

In my current search for these potential gems, my discoveries have been found among the words of political leaders, writers, historians, scientists, philosophers, thinkers, world citizens and activists of all kinds.

Once found, I have carved, chiseled and sculptured them into poems that I present to you in *Sculptum Est Prosa, Volume 4 – The Voices of the Oceans and Trees.*

Preface

This is an excerpt of a school report written six years ago by my grand-daughter when she was in 5th grade living in Salt Lake City.

> Have you ever looked outside on a January day? Well, lately it has been really bad. You can barely see about 2-3 miles away. If you hiked to the top of any mountain, higher than the smog around the valley, you would see a big grey cloud of pollution like a blanket covering the city. The pollution is 57% because of cars. This **MUST** be stopped!
>
> There are many reasons why the bad air quality must be stopped. One is bad health. Babies are born dead or are really sick. The elderly are in great risk of death as well as those with respiratory diseases. Certainly the residents of Salt Lake City deserve better air quality.

—By Cameron Pearl

...if these poems don't make you cry...you have no heart.

"I, one man alone
Was making ready
the battle to endure
Of the journey
And of the pity it involved

O memory
That wrote down what I saw
Trust me to this arduous road
If I have truly understood your words

Your soul is burdened
With that cowardice
Which often weighs
So heavily on man

All the way down
I entered this deep and rugged road."

—Dante,
The Divine Comedy, Canto 2

"...the most astonishing thing about trees is how social they are. The trees in a forest care for each other, sometimes even going as far as to nourish the stump of a felled tree for centuries after it was cut down by feeding sugars and other nutrients, and so keeping it alive."

—Peter Wohlleben,
The Hidden Life of Trees

I

the sound of trees

the branches rise
the branches fall
i hear their sounds as i sleep…
i hear their hearts beat

we transport
we produce
i hear the sound of blades
i hear their heart beat fade

the bark is stripped
i see their limbs bleed
look into my eyes…into my tears
it's gone far beyond what i can endure

does the dragon have a heart
can this be reconciled
between dionysus and apollo
in the vicissitudes of our soul

The glaciers and glacial lakes in the Himalayas provide water for about ten percent of the world's population…but the glaciers are melting at an increasing rate…endangering the life and property of the thousands of people residing below the lakes.

Climate change disproportionately affects the most vulnerable and marginalized people around the world; the people who are least responsible for the crisis…

I I

the mountains wail

cracks and reforms
in my veiled evening walk…
distant thoughts…
of an innocent child

from the violent insight
through the jagged leaves
i stand beneath a darkened tree
where pain and scars push me to my knees

blocking my sight
from the heavens and the stars
bring me my bow of burning gold
bring me my arrows of desire

in moments created new
for delusion interwoven
in a cavernous earth
of labyrinthine intricacy

from my left foot
a blackened cloud
all falling toward the center
in dire ruin, the mountains wail

"In this materialist phase of civilization where the visionary Garden of Eden has faded and the senses have rolled themselves in fear and the flat earth has become a ball...have the Sons of Ozoth given us artificial riches and scorn and trouble and sorrow, shutting the moon and stars and trees?"

—William Blake

I I I

bones of solitude

the sea throws it back to the shore
a weather in the quarter of the veins
i who was shapeless as the water
the waters of the heart

pushing in their tides
i reached the curving brink
of a steep bank of the darkened sea...
of scattered bottles and discarded cans

there is grass between the cracks
growing up from the temple floor
to this point of spacelessness
mingled and heaped in a rusty bin

i dare you make this journey
to the low fords of the ocean
where the clouds are inverted
and ancient nights have fled

deep down into the abyss
the trembling ages will behold
burning pebbles on the enraged beach
as bones of solitude tremble and weep

"The veil of human miseries is woven over the Ocean, From the Atlantic to the Great South Sea, the Erythrean...

...who creeps into State Government like a caterpillar to destroy, to cast off the idiot Questioner who is always questioning, but never capable of answering, who sits with a sly grin Silent plotting when to question like a thief in a cave...

Who publishes doubt and calls it knowledge: whose Science is Despair, whose pretense to knowledge is envy: whose whole Science is to destroy the wisdom of ages to gratify ravenous envy,

That rages round him like a Wolf day & night without rest. He smiles with condescension..."

—William Blake

IV

blood ocean

i found plastic
beneath the ocean floor
the dead forests, dead rivers
dead land upon the fatal brook

all vanished
from my sight
as i sit by a stream
under crying trees

listening
to their unheard speeches
tall and silent…
do you even understand

tortuous streets and dreariness
top hats of bureaucrats
as badgers scratch
the river's feet

the frosty silence…
agony in this stony place
my tenth finger emerges
from beneath this blood ocean floor

"Just this year, huge forest fires exacerbated by climate change have devastated vast areas of land in Australia and killed millions of animals. Recent research shows that the world's oceans are absorbing as much heat as that generated by five atomic bombs every second.

Toxic smog continues to choke India's cities despite repeated promises of cleaner air from the government, and the last decade was the warmest in recorded history."

—Mark Thompson and Max Foster

V

the sky is less grand

twenty-seven folds of opaqueness
in the north
solid and unfathomable
permitting evil…and without end

these are the starry voids of night
in the depths of caverns
amidst a red-hot globe
sunk down with fright

a fire is glowing
secretly celebrated by artificial riches…
the daylight's fading…
and the air is darkening

round, burning
deep as if sinking
from bosom into the deep
racing to the cliff with abandon

in pangs i hovered
i trembled and i wept…
the heat of this fire hath sadness
and the sky is less grand…as it shuts down

"The industrial revolution that first married economic growth with burning fossil fuels occurred in 18th-century Britain. The explosion of economic activity that marked the post-war period known as the "Great Acceleration" caused emissions to soar, and it largely took place in the Global North. That's why richer countries such as the US and UK, which industrialized earlier, bear a bigger burden of responsibility for historical emissions.

Developing regions in Africa, Asia and Latin America often bear the brunt of climate and ecological catastrophes, despite having contributed the least to them."

—Heather Alberro

V I

broken sun

until our wood is gone
the food and water too
taking us to where
no human has ever stood

this…the track we are on
in the garden…
un-adored…
incoherently absorbed

plunging like a waterfall…
the bleeding has begun
the spring has unraveled…
and man has broken the sun

"Having discovered subterranean reserves of energy, humans begin to change the composition of the atmosphere...This, in turn, alters the climate and the chemistry of the oceans."

—Elizabeth Kolbert,
The Sixth Extinction:
An Unnatural History

VII

science in despair

a world's raging waters
and sultry wastes
loud groans
beneath the poisoned void

stilted plants
sit in silent lament
the oceans've fled…
while continent's tremble

a wintry globe descends
deform'd into indefinite space
ungovernable in its fury
shutting the sun and moon

science in despair
a pretense to knowledge…
the criminals are fiddling
as we acidify and burn

"No creature has ever altered life on the planet in this way
before...those of us alive today not only are witnessing one
of the rarest events in life's history, we are also causing it...
Human activity has transformed between a third and a
half of the land surface of the planet."

—Elizabeth Kolbert

VIII

the thread

the thread
has been broken
symptoms unbounded…
the clouds unfold

thru albion's forests…
dark gleams and molten ore
'the heaves…the iron cliffs
the wind of Beulah scream'

unrooting the rocks and hills
snared and caught and taken
the rules
have abruptly changed

traits lethal
the old's given way
our greatest works left behind
compressed in sediment

sculptures and books
monuments and museums
dust…as thin
as the paper i am writing on

every plant that's grown
sits in silent lament
the oceans've fled…
continent's displaced

a world of raging waters
sultry wastes
and a poisoned void…
groans beneath the iron forge

trembling…
she weeps over the space
a wintry globe descends
deformed into indefinite space

ungovernable in fury
shutting the sun and moon
raging like a wolf
a state of dismal woe

'altered the poles of the world…
rintrah reared up walls of rocks
and poured rivers and moats of fire
bent down to the bosom of death'

what was underneath
soon seem'd above
a cloudy heaven
mingled with stormy seas

in the loudest ruin
hardening into bone
walls of rocks
against the surging flood

the veil of misery
woven …
formless…the straining force
wrests from the earth…submerged in its fate

"...our soaring emissions are never blamed on anything as concrete as the fossil fuel corporations that work furiously to block all serious attempts to regulate emissions, and certainly not on the economic model that demands that these companies put profit before the health of the natural systems upon which all life depends."

—Naomi Klein

IX

mouth of a hundred lips

bitumen
from the alberta sands
coal
from our mountain'd blast

while doubling down
bankers gamble
monetizing nature
villains vague and hidden threats

strangers
sell the wind
an earth skinned alive
and the theft of the sky

from this tear-drenched land
a wind arose
upon the brink
of grief's abysmal valley

into the sightless world
a snowflake wept
the islands scarred
the tempest strikes

time in the hour-less houses
shaking the sea-hatched skull
all-hollowed men weep
and stones become shadows

and the tattered dress
the river of hunger
the heart of ash
its ruptured voice…

voice of an old book
mouth of a hundred lips
that at once…
the air devours

"Can you provide an example of an ecosystem on which was laid down a barrage of poisons, and terrible and unexpected consequences for human beings were not the result?"

—Sandra Steingraber

X

invading knives

nations stare at their shoes
trapped in linear speech
spray saltwater skyward
to brighten the clouds

nature responds

phaetons…
you dare to regulate the sun
ye shall be…
struck down by zeus

'words spelled out
in somber colors
inscribed along the ledge
above a gate'

you emptied the fonts
of holy water
and filled it full
with toxin and bloodstained ink

as mountains burn
bedrocks are blasted
glaciers bleed
on a dying acidified sea

o' how she weeps
there are no frogs
no amphibians or coral reefs
seagrasses or mangroves

we attack their armor
as ferns shadows
of spattered crystal
invade our sword

as the primal ivy
puts a hand of blue
on the planet's silence
of land cut to pieces

of blood in the branches
by our invading knives...
will time's secret mouth
give this day its hollowness

"*In the kingdom of ends everything has
either a price or a dignity.*"

—Emanuel Kant

XI

the rape of the imaginary

a milky
geoengineered ceiling
gazing down
into techno wizardry

lopping off mountaintops
scraping off boreal forests
nature…
a bottomless vending machine

the trampling, crushing
torched fields, winding roads
weaved into ash…
the rape of the imaginary

"…*the many quotidian activities we perform just to get on with our personal lives. Those activities have made us the most destructive species in the history of life.*"

—E.O. Wilson

XII

language of the earth

blue water
belonging to no one
beyond repair
like the gradual dimming of light

unyoke our steaming horses
the soil is bare
in a forest of ghosts…
only the akohekoe survives

with the sun in a golden cup
leaf over leaf
dawn-branch in the sky…
my earth is turning ashen

just the sounds of sighs
rising and trembling
through the timeless air
where clouds are cursed by thunder

suffering barren waters
where turtles nibble
come unto sea-struck towers
weep when the weather howls

seaports by a drunken shore
the bitter finger of the wind…
may a humble planet labor
to answer the night hollow in song

a ship in unmoving waters
languishing…
longing for its breath
in the language of the earth

"Once the Arctic melts, there's no way to freeze it back up again, not in human time...we're at something like peak human right now, and it would be a worthy task to try to stay there — to spread the benefits of the last hundred years in diet and public health across geography and class, and to try to ward off the side effects of twentieth-century progress before it compromises twenty-first-century lives."

—Bill McKibben

XIII

stones of arauca

stars float along the void
quickening for the riddled sea
upon the battered…
the scarred and burned

a wild sheep
faraway…
licks the frozen color of stone
don't you hear the bleating

the blue squall
in whose hands
the moon is a wineglass…
don't you see the flock

touching the wave
with its empty ring
everything…
devoured in the dust

stones of arauca
an unleashed fluvial
where wilderness has no words
in the unwritten pages

in the farthest
and deepest waters
the grasses will rise…
as the arctic melts

"...*global warming is only part of a much larger environmental and social crisis that compels us to reflect on the values and direction of our now global civilization.*"

—David R. Loy

XIV

broken strains

te urewera
i am the river
and the river is me

i am the rain forest
manipulated
the winds pass over

the charm dissolved
a burning fire
of irreversibility

morning
stolen upon the night
earth's womb tightens

melting the darkness
rising senses chasing…
ignorance bearing its broken strains

"What was a metaphor up to now – that even the stones cried out in pain in the face of the miseries humans had inflicted on them – has become literal."

—Bruno Latour, *Facing Gaia*

XV

the third circle

as an opera
with neither score
nor ending
imposing its iron cage

there are no spectators
there is no shore
in muted raw obstinance
even the stones cry out in pain

earth is trembling
it shifts and moves
in its restless orbit
between what is and what must be

that lawless stream
dialectically immersed
in a metamorphic zone
where the shapeshifters reside

infinite spaces
of constant commotion
fragile spaces
and overlapping waves

in the morning wind
i hear a distant bell
my poem is interrupted...
we have entered the third circle of hell

"*...we will find ourselves, in the face of our frontal collision with Gaia...*
Our nightmares assail us while we are wide awake."

—Deborah Danowski

XVI

the muddle is gaia

tragedy from a distant shore
leaves no history behind
from its deep plates
to its envelope of air

an airy
and unplastered cabin
where a goddess
trails her garments

the ridges of mountains
celestial parts of terrestrial music
where few are the ears
that hear

have we crossed the threshold
beyond that which we cannot curb
beyond what we cannot confine
what do you do…after you stop pretending

everything's in motion
the paradox
the bewildered onlookers
in this…the muddle of gaia

"Stinging the soul to wailing
The infernal storm
Eternal in its rage"

—Dante

XVII

the final verse

invisible characters
reversing the order
entangled, blurred and muddled…
the paradox of the contradictory

black clouds wrapping their wings
fell with the dawn
i saw olympus…
the ocean outside the earth

the hierarchy of agents
the monstrous and the shameless
how will you draw the line
how will you fight that which resists even thought

but the final verse
is always the trees
let the drum be brought forth
into a silent seamless world

the unfolding equations
a circle of mighty stones
the oceans and crustal rocks
the extermination by sword

fiction has vanished
the weight of ice
rests on the fuselage
of tree and stone

once more the rhythm
vibrates underfoot
in held-back silence
as the voice of earth trembles

"...the gas companies are continuing to drill, leak, and pour billions of dollars into new infrastructure...doubling down on the stuff that is causing the crisis in the first place...[as we] look for a split second and then we look away."

—Naomi Klein

XVIII

magical thinking

buzzing chainsaws
toppling trees
decapitated mountains
drowned valleys and strip-mined hills

weather futures
phony numbers
carbon cowboys
technological schemes...

the imponderable calamity...
dried out oceans
magical thinking
modifying clouds

i scream...
a roof is not a sky
in a voice like a bayonet
as the water is poisoned and fracked

the intoxicating frenzy
ice shelves collapse
the black void beneath me
swallowing everything...even sound

"*In a sane world, this cluster of disasters, layered on top of the larger climate crisis, would have prompted significant political change. Caps and moratoriums would have been issued, and the shift away from extreme energy would have begun. The fact that nothing of the sort has happened, and that permits and leases are still being handed out for ever more dangerous extractive activities, is at least partly due to old-fashioned corruption — of both the legal and illegal varieties.*"

—Naomi Klein

XIX

shattered

the swans, the muskrats
and trees
coated in black

handfuls of nothing
a petroleum sheen
a fluttering horizon

footsteps
with no land
naked banks

where birds
once strut to watch
a sea as thick as blood

glances of life
irretrievable
killed and broken in pieces

how tracelessly
you have gone away
a living world is shattered

"...it is as though the threads of tragedy were woven not just by the Olympian gods of long ago but by all the agents from the beginning of time. This is the story of the Anthropocene: a truly Oedipal myth.

And, unlike Oedipus, who was blind to his own actions for so long, as we face the revelation of past errors we must resist the temptation to blind ourselves anew: we must agree to look at them head on, in order to be able to face what is coming toward us with our eyes wide open."

—Bruno Latour, *Facing Gaia*

X X

the bleeding trees

we seek to understand
the order of the earth
in labyrinthine forms
beyond the unlearn-ed myths

the oceans advance
born in the tempest
replacing the course of time
suspended amid the senseless

threads of tragedy
networks intermingled
tracing the loops…
of the mutually entangled

a boundary on nature
no matter where i move
or turn my eyes
no matter where i gaze

in the veiled forests
the night is throbbing…
in the round of rain
the earth is sinking

the forest of maytens
whose green threads weep
the absence of future
and the bleeding trees

"A glacier is essentially suspended energy, suspended force. It is time, in that sense, life, frozen in time. But now, these frozen rivers of time are themselves running out of time. The planet's ecosystems, now pushed far beyond their capacity to adapt to human-generated traumas and stresses, are in a state of free fall."

—Dahr Jamail, *The End of Ice*

XXI

the fuse is lit

enmity turns out to be
infinitely broadened…
of the time that is passing
of time compressed

suspended energy
once frozen in time
vanishing…
unstoppably melting

lives…
in a world of wounds
the anthropogenic disruption…
touches the sphere of eternity

mountain's faces rippled
gullies strain skyward
the collapse is unstoppable
the fuse is lit

day is wreathed
in what summer lost
its thread is spun
in violent, raging and unchecked winds

"*Extraction is taking. Actually, extraction is stealing – it is taking without consent, without thought, care or even knowledge of the impacts that extractions has on the other living things in that environment.*"

—Leanne Betasamosake Simpson,
As We Have Always Done

XXII

dispossession

without permission
without consent
in your cunning, removed
and dispossessed

stolen, sub-divided and sold
beaches, bays, peninsulas
ceremonial sites
and nesting spots

i see the world
where sound is gone
the teaching rocks
and the breeding grounds

"While indigenous thinkers have always been strongly rooted in place, we have also always seen the complicated ways our existence is intrinsically linked to and is influencing global phenomena..."

—Leanne Betasamosake Simpson,
As We Have Always Done

XXIII

nanabush (1)

nanabush
walked the earth twice
to understand our place

the ancient one
gnarled root hidden deep
origin unbeheld

nanabush
the human and non-human
the stories, the ceremonies and the songs

then the rising and falling
of ancient fountains
broke open...stone by stone

do you recognize him
air full of places you once absorbed
the ceremonial embers still burning in his hands

nanabush...stayed in the forest
a bear among the bears
a bird among the birds

"[climate change deniers] often have a veneer of plausibility,
but scratch the surface, and you witness a sleight of hand,
where climate projections are lowballed; climate change
impacts, damages, and costs are underestimated…"

—Michael Mann,
The Madhouse Effect

XXIV

the roses are painted grey

at the edge of a cliff
distortion, denial
and confusion

dark money
sleight of hand
disinformation and delay

the roses are painted grey

placing mirrors in space
painting rooftops white
abstract models and magic tricks

corroding space
inversion between figure and ground
the ambiented becomes the ambient

the roses are painted grey

"*the revolution has already occurred…the events we have to cope with do not lie in the future, but largely in the past… Whatever we do now, the threat will remain with us for centuries, for millennia.*"

—Bruno Latour

XXV

slow violence

slow violence
an ecological desert
a whirling storm

a ferocious corrosion
of time and space

nightmares assail us
in the sweep of the black wind
across the filthy waves

a world hollowed out
along shores of plastic and waste

counter-temperatures clash
and tear through forests
like a ruthless invader

a monstrous predator of our own
a species as hypnotized prey

suicidal vertigo
the forest-world suffocates
a fall of celestial layers

only the naked man shall understand
the stage of the ice
the once solid ocean

our collision with gaia
the pound of lava
our towns on a wheel of fire

"How are we to account for the problem of climate change attribution, and how to speak of deviation from the norm if the norm itself is changing with every new year?

Hotter and colder, drier and wetter, faster and slower, clearer and darker; now more, now less sensitivity or reflectivity. The instability affects time, quantities, qualities, measures and scales themselves; it also corrodes space."

—Deborah Danowski, *The Ends of the World*

XXVI

this day in its hollowness

alarms sounded
into a policy of paralysis…
an ignorance of uncertainty

the misinformed deliberate
while meanings disintegrate
into inexhaustible illusions

a megaphone screams
smears and untruths…
the betrayal of earth

impoverished…defenseless
defiled and diminished
the forgetfulness of being

in an austral panic
this day in its hollowness…
our sphere slowly sinks into your shadow

"...the next generations will have to survive in an impover-
ished, sordid environment; an ecological desert , a socio-
logical hell...

We are therefore not only dealing with a "crisis" in time
and space, but a ferocious corrosion of time and space...

Apparently, then, we find ourselves not only on the verge
of a return to a "pre-modern condition," but we will find
ourselves, in the face of our frontal collision with Gaia, even
more defenseless than so-called "primitive man" found
itself before the power of Nature.

Our nightmares assail us while we are wide awake."

—Deborah Danowski

XXVII

it used to be

the meadows
are no longer green
the sky
is no longer blue

we have followed
those inverted images
created by
the subtraction of subjects

conjured through
and kept at bay
by an animalization
of the mask of the spirit-dancer

reciprocally…
a dehumanization
crushed
by a falling sky

from this double movement
there are souls everywhere
like pilgrims in a fable
swallowed up and lost

nights dark
beyond darkness
and the days
more gray

trunks of trees
charred and limbless
stretching away
on every side

the long gray dusks
the long gray dawns
where the shape of a city
once stood

like a charcoal drawing
sketched across the waste
trekking the dried floor
of a mineral sea

tattered gods
slouching in rags
lay cracked and broken
fallen crystal

the world
shrinking down
about a raw core
of parsible entities

borrowed time
and borrowed world
and borrowed eyes
with which to sorrow it

'is it blue
the sea
i don't know
it used to be'

"*Nights dark beyond darkness and the days more gray each one than what had gone before. Like pilgrims in a fable swallowed up and lost among the inward parts of some granitic beast. It swung its head from side to side and then gave out a low moan and turned and lurched away and loped soundlessly into the dark.*

Barren, silent, godless…the long gray dusks, the long gray dawns. Charred and limbless trunks of trees stretching away on every side... where the shape of a city stood in the grayness like a charcoal drawing sketched across the waste."

—Cormac McCarthy, *The Road*

XXVIII

the chime travels

barren and silent
i awoke in the dark
bull drums beating
somewhere in the low dark hills

an invisible moon
nights slightly less black
by day...
a banished sun circled

then the wind shifted
dreams once rich in color
like entombed ancient frescoes
suddenly exposed to light of day

creedless shells of men
tottering down the causeways
pretending to enter a secret gate
which is and will forever be, unlocked

claims lofty and empty
as an abandoned cathedral
their fatal shadows
and vehement play of causes

as the wheel turns on its axis
passing objects and hues
in the midst of the irrational...
as they drown, the chime travels

like a grieving mother
her lamp shining…
looking at the edge of the world
across the waste paths of feral fire

sorry it's not blue
her feet press on their emptiness
where time was the velocity and flurry
the denier's insolence…the frailty revealed

the sacred idiom
shorn of referents
from a planet
that no longer exists

"...the more I question scientists, the more scared I get. Because this story does add up, and its message is that we are interfering with the fundamental processes that make Earth habitable.

Climate is an angry beast, and we are poking it with sticks."

—Fred Pearce,
With Speed and Violence

XIX

the flower is silent

a manhood of ending
falling steadily and quick
breaking the threads
that bind life to life

the cadaverous gravels
in the ancient dark beyond
a spring without voices
hands that have no tears

that which walk by us still
with all its anger
this obliteration of the color
where once a tree was wearing red

the wide land, the wilderness
filled with murmurs, arms' mouths
a mute syllable kept burning
until the meadows shook

i went between the streets
saw the soft underbelly
the sheet of antarctic's ice
ripped open before my eyes

the lock is broken
vulnerable to forcings
a woven mat
that nature never invented

was then an ulcerous twilight
a leprosarium
engulfed in shadows
its gathering of light repulsed

the land, oceans and cities
as a shaken stone
the flower is silent
the earth is broken

"There is chaos out there, and we should be afraid. statistical models of climate, sophisticated though they undoubtedly are, badly underestimate the forces of change...the modelers are growing ever more fearful about what might really lie out there...

The more I learn...the more I question scientists, the more scared I get. Because this story does add up, and its message is that we are interfering with the fundamental processes that make Earth habitable."

—Fred.Pearce,
With Speed and Violence

XXX

blood and stone

chaos shrieks
riding the sea light
destruction, picked by birds
'sicklied o'er with the pale cast of thought'

childish man under them
his huge globe a toy
childish man interfering
on a sunken path

like an angry beast
poked with sharpened sticks...
chemicals in the arctic air
raining mercury...melting trees

'brays through the jawbone
dark with contagion'
into the icy breath of death
i am... deformity itself

a roar amid the dream
a rainless rainforest
pesticides and the acid haze
the dish is boiled... with blood and stone

"Fifty- five million years ago, more than a trillion tons of methane burst from the ocean, sending temperatures soaring by up to 18°F extinguishing two thirds of the species in the ocean depths, and causing a major evolutionary shock at the surface.

The story, while from long ago, is a reminder that methane lurks in prodigious quantities in many parts of the planet — not just in frozen bogs — and that one day it could be liberated in catastrophic quantities."

—Fred Pearce

XXXI

scarred

scarred
divided into fragments
the reindeer have fled
the bears have been hunted

pipelines, roads, pylons
littered with abandoned drums
the lake of bodies...
mingled and heaped in a bin

half-built railways
bonerailed and masterless
shrouded in black smoke
acid pitted pteropods

predators break the weakened shells
as lakes crack open
a brass and bodiless image...
as we enter terra incognita

"...the young women in Bangladesh's firetrap factories who make the clothes on our bodies, or the children in the Democratic Republic of the Congo whose lungs are filled with dust from mining cobalt for [our] phones. Ours is an economy of ghosts, of deliberate blindness."

—Naomi Klein

XXXII

sacrificial zones

leaders torch the planet
with defiant glee
paid-off lobbyists
the denier movement's disbelief

hubris in the face of ignorance
forces uncomprehended…
disinformation, obfuscation
and straight-up lies

children mining cobalt
lungs and dust…
will the dirt recede
before my prophetical scream

sacrificial zones
dot the globe
in shallowness…in rootlessness
this shredded state of lifelessness

collapsing mythologies
stolen and poisoned lands
an approaching wave
sprawled in its ruin

squall lines of ash
dark with contagion
sketched like a paper scrim
upon the pall of soot

"Enough smoke has descended to turn the sky from peri-winkle blue to this low, unbroken white. Enough smoke to reflect a good portion of the sun's heat back into space, artificially pushing temperatures down. Enough smoke to transform the sun itself into an angry pinpoint of red fire surrounded by a strange halo, unable to burn through the relentless haze. Enough smoke to blot out the stars. Enough smoke to absorb any possible sunsets."

—Naomi Klein,
*On Fire: The Burning Case
for a Green New Deal*

XXXIII

the relentless haze

nature revealed
wounded, broken and grey
no longer abusable
the theft is under way

in rocks, mountains and streams
hard limits have been hit
the heavens are naked
blood's coated…icy thick

we have cracked open
the heart of it
children discard what's broken
the dancing's dreary, the music's counterfeit

they came
with a language without words
in the fog of thin hope
silenced even the singing of birds

pages in water…
spinning the day
broken sounds with lies
that bleed across this page

smoke has transformed
the sun's once soothing blaze
into a slow-dying glow
burning through the relentless haze

grey truth
in dreams from disdain to tears
i turn my restless head...
the wearer of the robe has disappeared

"We don't even know what we are losing. We don't understand what a loss of biodiversity fully means...We are losing things before we actually know, fully what we are losing."

—Dr. Laurie Raymundo,
University of Guam Marine Lab

XXXIV

scars of an injured world

the ocean's poem
pressing the pulse of the life
the clicking sounds
of fish biting coral

the water crackles
waves like a forest…
intricately woven
in this web of life

as surroundings fall silent
as time slips away
to when there is no more coral
and there are no more fish

there's a hollow mist
the sea sweeps on
someone is singing…
a song no one can hear

the world is broken
a black raven is cawing
giving voice to sorrow
giving voice to a prophetic cry

an outburst of contempt
of defiant sorrow
a violent wound
in every particle of the air

like the moon's seed
like the stars' blood
like the sun's tears...
and the scars of an injured world

*"Planet Earth is becoming hazier;
the wild blue yonder is not so blue."*

—Fed Pearce,
With Speed and Violence

XXXV

i wander this sad world

the levels are rising...
the dance floors are full
by Miami's skyline
on the edge of the sea

the demons have arrived
with ropes and cages
the destruction is rising...
the cloudless sky is split

i wander this sad world

in another land
acid fog
is trapped in layers
being swallowed by the sea

blaring cries
through the vertical cliffs...
highways are buckling
thickets crumple to ash

i wander this sad world

the pearl disappears
beneath furious waves...
the trees are gone
the dry soil is baked

that first cry opens the door
you breathe it in
but within you it hardens
then it's gone.

i wander this sad world

*"...we are facing the most massive wave of
extinction in 65 million years..."*

—The Dalai Lama

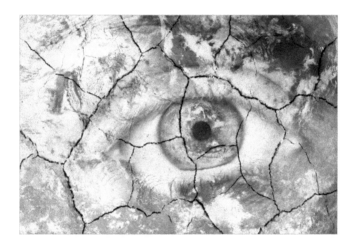

*"The biosphere, our planetary life-support system
can no longer support our levels of exploitation."*

—John Stanley

XXXVI

nanabush (2)

nanabush visits
the rivers and lakes
the animals and spirits
the mountains and the plains

and in his reflection...
saw in all directions
a shattered spring
grief with disheveled hands

a countryside of pain
taken without consent
without thought...
without care

kanien'keh'a:ka pines
crushed in the storm
a wrathful rose
of stone and wounds

tear out the alter ghost
shed his arena of might
restore the majesty
and guard the cycle of dawn

"We are not standing at the threshold of dangerous climate change. We passed through that door decades ago."

—Phillip Sutton, David Spratt,
Climate Code Red (2008)

"Three-quarters of a century since global warming was first recognized as a problem, we have made no meaningful adjustment to our production or consumption of energy to account for it and protect ourselves."

—David Wallace-Wells,
The Uninhabitable Earth

XXXVII

the crystal is bled

black hat'd
snow covered mountains…
forests ripped up
awakened in gray

feeding the dense
sludge from the mines
a black soup
woven in blood

angus cows stagger
like broken toys
dark eyes are burning
as tags melt to their ears

carved out birds
blunted striking throats
piercing the split sky
in weed and heel

the oceans
hot, sour, and breathless
the glanded morrow
the staked and the fallow

i scream treason
against a broken planet
flames patterned in lacquer
with doom in the bulb

grim purgatory before you
the crystal is bled
the dry world's lever
is faltering now...

MERCURY AND THE WOODMAN

"One legacy of the environmentalist creed that long prized
the natural world as an otherworldly retreat is that we see
its degradation as a sequestered story, unfolding separately
from our own modern lives — so separately that the degra-
dation acquires the comfortable contours of parable, like
pages from Aesop, aestheticized even when we know the
losses as tragedy."

—David Wallace-Wells,
The Uninhabitable Earth

XXXIII

the dance of the dream-led masses

as if cascades
in their slowness
as if a fairy tale...
an anthology of delusions

an arctic saga unfolding
an evolutionary reset
down along a rough, strange path
where the marsh's vapers are hidden

like pages from a fable
the degradation
as a sequestered story
aestheticized...even when we know

civilizations swallowed
in a revenge of time
the disastrous rhythm
in a dance of the dream-led masses

"…we have now engineered as much ruin knowingly
as we ever managed in ignorance."

—David Wallace-Wells

XXXIX

twisted logic

my planet's pummeled
the cities are drowning
a gap that yawns so wide
between me and the silver chair

avalanches of devastation
unfolding so separately
that the degradation acquires
contours of a sacred parable

the rio grande
is a line traced
through a dry riverbed...
wildfires are burning across the west

input beyond equations
of half-ignorance and half -indifference
fatally complacent
and willfully deluded

a sliver of life
turning violently against us
transformed...like sunken ships
into underwater relics

beyond the villainy
of twisted logic
collapsing in the distance
beyond the revenge of time

"...the true cruelty of climate change...
can upend and turn violently against us everything
we have ever thought to be stable."

—David Wallace-Wells

X L

his grandmother's world

on an earth
where once upon a time
our political fatalism
and technological faith blurred

the cascading chaos
the true cruelty
exploitative empires...
where so many acres burned

pressing fossils
into petro
extracted from that muck
like lemon under a press

and a child will begin a story
about his grandmother's world...
when the river wasn't here
and a village once sat

"Where were you when the Berlin Wall fell? or Where were you on 9/11? Will it ever be possible to ask, in the same vein, Where were you at 400 ppm [parts per million]? or Where were you when the Larsen B ice shelf broke up?"

—Amitav Ghosh,
The Great Derangement

XLI

shadow of time

traces and portents
of an altered world
torn and bent

you try
to understand my poem
by counting the words

'postilions killed
at every stage
horses ridden to death
on every page'

somber forests
heartaches, vows
sobs and tears

clouds have gathered
the deluge pours
the sea snarls in its terrible wrath

the moon is cursed
and anathematized
our earth laughing
mocking our own mockery

the tiger is watching
the tiger is charging
a shock courses through you

he advances
there are shadows…
you are frozen…

a strangeness unfolds
shapes are forming
you do not see them
the uncanniness and lies

burning forests
hurricanes
teeth of savage stone

circle stung awake
we've taken
all there is to take

even stripped
the twelve-winded marrow
like a doomed anchor…
a seashell in the shadow of time

"With all their genius and with all their skill, they ran out of foresight and air and food and water and ideas…They went on playing politics until their world collapsed around them."

—Amitav Ghosh

XLII

rest robbed, my beast

hell in a horn of sulfur
and the cloven myth…
a serpent fiddling
in the shaping time

the greenery once dense
where man casts his years
as the snake his slough…
a wild delight ran through

as if we have no debt
neither allegiance nor respect
wanting more
until there is no more to steal

they wrestled and raged
sharp stones were hurled
vengeance-crazed
void without image

his gods are cast back
he's no course to set
only to drift too long
and wait and wait and wait

chaff, rolled into balls
the mythological exterior
lies on the forest's moss
pine at its trunk's shadow

'clips short the gesture of breath
die in red feathers
when the flying's heaven's cut
lie dry, rest robbed, my beast'

"...extractive capitalism has run its course...we are faltering now,
and the human game has indeed begun to play itself out."

—Bill McKibben

XLIII

calls with the wind

bludgeoned sundown
storm at her heart
the cries fracture the night

abandoned and eyeless
a shade that's in hell
at thy road's end

the air is heavy
everything's cold
the trees no longer move

somber blood
pages of water…
and the muffled cries

refusal struck
beneath the waves…
beneath the agonized seas

beside a bowl of wounds and weeds
my eyes've been nailed…
staring wide open

*"we are at the place
of souls who lost
the good of intellect"*

—Dante

XLIV

the oceans and the trees

shrieks of lamentation
these sounds resounding
making me weep

pine needle
expanded and swelled
gods hold in the air

a sympathetic chord
seeks me and sobs
the mask is torn from the phantom

land burnt to the ground
turning glaciers into black
caramelized snow and smoke-shrouded views

like a sister…a beautiful mother
who once opened her arms in embrace
today she groans in travail

against ruthless exploiters…
the barren coral reefs
a billion animals are dead

smell the burning bottom of form
inhale acres of your shade
hang with beheaded veins

and let her eyelids fasten
locked into mortal combat
with the oceans and the trees

"Will an abstract idea of fairness be sufficient to undertake cuts on this scale in a world where the pursuit of self-interest is conceived of as the motor of the economy?"

—Amitov Ghosh,
The Great Derangement

XLV

this play's turned tragic

armed lifeboat politics
a malthusian correction
consumed in devouring scars
and, as for the oil...

military intrusion
war's been declared
congregating the clandestine rose
trampled by metals and gallops

unthinkable...
with power at the core
hear the cry of the earth
of the defenseless poor

the barbed fences
faces staring out
through the rampart
'shall the star-flanked seed be riddled'

recoiling in horror
at your own handiwork
watch the sun go down
through the smog and poisoned waters

playing politics
above the appalling ruin
great walls have fallen
breathing's stopped...this play's turned tragic

"What color is glory...
Through dead men's drums?"

—Dylan Thomas

XLVI

silenced

underwater cemeteries
bereft of color and life
twelve million acres
torched across the land

like stepping into a zone
where the echoes reach
beyond
what you thought you could see

shadows and images
where once appeared
intricate dapplings of light
oceans, rivers and lakes

endless iterations
of dust and images
the forests of stone
silencing…even the songs of the birds

"…at exactly the time when it has become clear that global warming is in every sense a collective predicament, humanity finds itself in the thrall of a dominant culture in which the idea of the collective has been exiled from politics, economics, and literature alike."

—Amitov Ghosh

XLVII

the unthinkable

rebellious logic knows no bounds
forests insert themselves
in our thoughts

there is no place
where the orderly expectations
hold unchallenged sway

in the sundarbans
tigers are everywhere
and nowhere

disclosing nothing
of the uncanny intimacy
we are confronted suddenly

imagining the unthinkable
over vast gaps
in time and space

the void
populous and the powerless
seasonless, herbless, treeless, manless, lifeless

"...our common home is like a sister with whom we share our life and a beautiful mother who opens her arms to embrace us. This sister now cries out to us because of the harm we have inflicted on her by our irresponsible use..."

—Pope Francis, *Laudato Si:*
On Care for Our Common Home

XLVIII

these tears

the window is closing
the die is cast
i am numb
questions wrestle inside me

go ahead
pretend
that the world is not unraveling
the terrible, wounded beauty

these tears…
but a small ceremony
touching everything
i see and do

"...we have changed the very chemistry of the planet, we have
altered the biosystems

we have changed the topography, and even the geological
structure of the planet

structures and functions that have taken hundreds of millions
and even billions of year to bring into existence."

—Thomas Berry,
The Dream of the Earth

XLIX

o, children of the world

and in you the light
old as the shadow
a branch of cedron
with an aroma that stuns

has then the chain
of the pleiades broken
taken pieces of moon
devoured this river with twilight

but o, children of the world
of all the many changing things
in dreariness…i ask
has the dancing whirled past us

"*Rintrah rear'd up walls of rocks and pour'd rivers &
moats of fire round the walls: to throw banks of sand
around the fiery flaming harrow in labyrinthine forms.
And brooks between to intercede the meadows in their
course. Chaos & ancient night fled from beneath the fiery
Harrow: The Harrow cast thick flames & orb'd us round
in concave fire...*"

—William Blake, *Milton*

L

doomed deniers

the woods of arcady are dead
the blood is spilled
while doomed deniers
stand before you

eager in their schemes
amid the wreckage
of fallen limbs
their wind-turned statements...melt in air

as lunatics
make up words
take a whole mouthful
and spit'm out

stirner laughed in the alley
damocles cames swiftly
as rooks disappear
and larks no longer sing

*"I see the world crumbling beneath my feet
with the weight of global capitalism..."*

—Leanne Betasamosake Simpson

L I

our children's dream

the muskrat's paw of dirt
is buried
beneath fractured pillars
where our children once dreamed

i shall patiently search
for softer patterns
came a voice from the well
a well…deeper than history

michi saagiig nishnaabeg…
our rivers and lakes
our migratory salmon
once respected and honored

biskaabiiyang…
our clan expanded and contracted
like a beating heart
the working of lungs

the flux
its changing forms
a relationship with forces
seamlessly joined to my body

nishnaabemowin…
it linked my beating heart
to the beating river
that flowed through this land

they came…
disturbed and dishonored
until moy e-kistawet
the echo is gone

subtle waves of disruption
our land no longer has sound
the water has dried
even the splash has gone

"No green leaves, but rather black in color
No smooth branches, but twisted and entangled
No fruit, but thorns of poison instead"

—Dante

LII

the shackled majesty

from that splintered trunk
a mixture poured
of words and blood
fire from a frozen cloud

it's two minutes to midnight
and bamboos are speaking
their sound as if weeping...
the flora and fauna are dying

the constant horror
of your own conscience
staring into your own face
in a coat of many-colored fictions

will fear save us
as we feel the long pulsation
as we mask our past
in the ebb and flow of endless motion

looking into a yellow grave
of sand and sea
into waves of extinction
between our heartbeat and our humanity

calling for color
as this majestic beauty
melts before our eyes
the mute voice of the drums...the shackled majesty

"*The first angel sounded his trumpet*
  and there came hail and fire mixed with blood
  and it was hurled down on the earth…
  A third of the earth was burned up
  a third of the trees were burned up
  and all the green grass was burned up"

—Revelation 8:7

LIII

planetary treason

the debate is over
humanity abandoned
a billion people
can't hold back the waters

the poor
are being swallowed
grandfathers' truths...
are possessed by shadows

where feet
once touched the earth
and promises were made...
the shadow's dire

conversing
until darkness is formed
your blood flows darkly
a raw wound, a bleeding rock

someday
our grandchildren will ask
when did the seasons stop
and the mammals and birds all die

every broken promise
every dream a nightmare
and every step back...
planetary treason

"Did you sing for the flower,
for the water
who's beauty
sing words to the stones
but the petals had no dew
those black waters had no words
the sun is dimmed in the day
and the stars at night."

—Pablo Neruda

LIV

regret

the earth folds back
on itself
the rivers are drained
and the valleys flooded

we have killed
ten thousand lakes
broke the mountains apart
we have lost our way

still there are winds that seem
like my wandering son
coming back to show me
how hermes once folded time

and the way up
has become the way down
the way forward
the way back

that the future
is a faded song
for those who are not yet here
to regret

"The time has now come...when we will listen or we will die...
The time has come to lower our voices to cease imposing
our mechanistic patterns on the biological processes of the
earth, to resist the impulse to control, to command to force,
to oppress and to begin quite humbly to follow the guidance
of the larger community on which all life depends."

—Thomas Berry,
The Dream of the Earth

LV

concrete and dreams

lower your voice
what's left
is 'pretend'…
even sound no longer bends

hold back
your children's tears
who once laughed and sang
at the mystique of the falling rain

the songs of the crickets
were skillfully cut
count the taken…
the mysteries forsaken

the birds are silent
their groves are cut…
and their handmade moon
fled past this shadow in bloom

today contradicts
every yesterday
a savage assault
hidden in an unmarked vault

and my longing grows
the edges are sharp
a landscape once green
is now of concrete and dreams

Epilogue

"*On their backs were vermiculate patterns*
that were maps of the world in its becoming
Maps and mazes

Of a thing which could not be put back
Not be made right again

In the deep glens where they lived
all things were older than man
and they hummed of mystery"

—Cormac McCarthy,
The Road

Bibliography

The prophetic books of William Blake: Milton— Blake, William

The Sixth Extinction: An Unnatural History—Kolbert, Elizabeth

Degrowth—Giacomo D'Alisa, Federico Demaria and Giorgos Kallis

This Changes Everything: Capitalism vs. The Climate—Klein, Naomi

Half-Earth: Our Planet's Fight for Life—Wilson, Edward O.

Ecodharma: Buddhist Teachings for the Ecological Crisis—Loy, David R.

Facing Gaia—Latour, Bruno

The End of Ice—Jamail

As We Have Always Done—Simpson

The Climate Emergency—Dorje

The Madhouse Effect—Mann, Michael

The Ends of the World—Danowski, Déborah

Dancing On Our Turtle's Back—Simpson

The Notebooks of Malte Laurids Brigge—Rilke, Rainer Maria

Silent Spring—Carson, Rachel

An American Sunrise—Joy Harjo

Walden—Thoreau, Henry David

Selected Writings—Emerson, Ralph Waldo

The Hidden Life of Trees—Wohleben

The Road—McCarthy, Cormac

A Word Without Ice—Pollack, Henry

The Outlaw Oceans: Journeys Across the Last Frontier—Urbina, Ian

With Speed and Violence—Pearce, Fred

On Fire: The Burning Case for a Green New Deal—Klein, Naomi

Falter—McKibben, Bill

The Uninhabitable Earth—Wallace-Wells, David

The Great Derangement—Amitov, Ghosh

Laudato Si: On Care for Our Common Home— Pope Francis

The Dream of the Earth— Thomas Berry

Climate Abandoned: We're on the Endangered Species List—Cody, Jill

Index

Lightning Source UK Ltd.
Milton Keynes UK
UKHW021139240520
363742UK00012B/539/J